M

MAR   2003

CH

"I've known rivers:

I've known rivers ancient as the world and older
than the flow of human blood in human veins.

My soul has grown deep like the rivers."

—LANGSTON HUGHES,
FROM "THE NEGRO SPEAKS OF RIVERS"

LANGSTON HUGHES: AFRICAN-AMERICAN POET

By Lucia Raatma

The Child's World

Published in the United States of America by The Child's World®
PO Box 326
Chanhassen, MN 55317-0326
800-599-READ
www.childsworld.com

The Child's World®: Mary Berendes, Publishing Director
Editorial Directions, Inc.: E. Russell Primm, Emily Dolbear, and Lucia Raatma,
Editors; Linda S. Koutris, Photo Selector; Dawn Friedman, Photo Researcher; Red Line Editorial,
Fact Researcher; Irene Keller, Copy Editor; Tim Griffin/IndexServ, Indexer;
Melissa McDaniel, Proofreader

Cover photograph: Portrait of Langston Hughes/ © Beinecke Rare Book & Manuscript Library,
Yale University Library

Interior photographs ©: AP/Wide World Photos: 19; Beinecke Rare Book & Manuscript Library,
Yale University Library: 2, 9, 12, 25, 26, 29, 30, 31, 32, 33, 35; Corbis: 15, 17; Bettmann/Corbis: 10, 16, 22;
Hulton-Deutsch Collection/Corbis: 14; E.O. Hoppe/Corbis: 24; Hulton Archive/Getty Images: 20, 21, 28;
James L. Allen/Library of Congress: 6; Library of Congress: 8; Schomburg Center for Research in Black
Culture, Prints & Photographs Division, The New York Public Library: 18, 23, 27; Houston Conwill, Rivers,
1991, mixed media, 16 x 17 1/2 inches/Schomburg Center for Research in Black Culture, Art & Artifacts
Division, The New York Public Library, Astor Lenox and Tilden Foundation: 36.

Library of Congress Cataloging-in-Publication Data
Raatma, Lucia.
Langston Hughes: African American author and poet / by Lucia Raatma.
p. cm. — (Journey to freedom)
Summary: Briefly introduces the life and accomplishments of Langston Hughes, an African American
writer who shared his views on racism through his poetry and prose, as well as through poetry readings.
Includes bibliographical references and index.
ISBN 1-56766-647-7 (library bound : alk. paper)
1. Hughes, Langston, 1902–1967—Juvenile literature. 2. Poets, American—20th century—Biography—
Juvenile literature. 3. African American poets—Biography—Juvenile literature. [1. Hughes, Langston,
1902–1967. 2. Poets, American. 3. African Americans—Biography.] I. Title. II. Series.
PS3515.U274 Z6975 2002
818'.5209—dc21
2001008119

Contents

LANGSTON HUGHES WAS ONE OF THE FINEST WRITERS IN THE HISTORY OF THE UNITED STATES. SOME OF HIS WORK WAS INFLUENCED BY THE RHYTHMS OF BLUES AND JAZZ MUSIC.

A Literary Voice

Langston Hughes is often called one of the greatest poets in the history of the United States. But Hughes was not only a poet. He also wrote novels and articles, plays and **librettos**, and even books for young people. He proved to be a strong literary voice, one who inspired his fellow African-Americans and influenced politicians throughout the world.

Hughes found his inspiration in the life he led and the people he met. He was also deeply moved by the words and the feel of **blues** and **jazz**, two musical styles that were popular when he was a young man. Often his poetry seemed to sing—soft and soothing and sometimes sad—just like a blues vocalist leaning against a piano in a crowded Harlem nightclub.

Throughout his career, Hughes wrote about the troubles African-Americans faced in the United States. He felt the effects of **racism**. Yet he had also tasted the fame and success that Americans of all backgrounds sometimes achieve. He wrote about other countries and their people. He wrote about dreams and disappointments. He wrote about life—complete with its happiness and its horrors, its surprises and its sorrow. And his work touched people from all walks of life.

JOPLIN, MISSOURI, IN 1900. LANGSTON HUGHES WAS BORN IN THIS CITY, BUT HIS CHILDHOOD WAS MARKED BY FREQUENT MOVES AND UNHAPPINESS.

The Young Mind

On February 1, 1902, James Langston Hughes was born in Joplin, Missouri. He was named for his father, James Nathaniel Hughes, as well as his mother, Carolina (Carrie) Langston Hughes, and he was known by his middle name. Langston did not have an easy childhood. In fact, his young life was marked by family unhappiness and frequent moves to new homes.

At this time in the United States, African-Americans were not treated equally or with respect by whites. In many places, blacks and whites were **segregated**. Blacks and whites had separate waiting rooms; separate areas in buses, restaurants, and theaters; and even separate water fountains. African-Americans were denied certain jobs and were frequently paid less than white workers.

YOUNG LANGSTON HUGHES AND HIS MOTHER, CARRIE. LANGSTON SPENT MUCH OF HIS BOYHOOD SEPARATED FROM HER.

IN THE EARLY PART OF THE TWENTIETH CENTURY, DURING MOST OF
HUGHES'S LIFE, SEGREGATION KEPT BLACKS AND WHITES APART. FROM AN
EARLY AGE, HUGHES NEW THAT THE WORLD COULD BE AN UNFAIR PLACE.

James Hughes experienced this unfairness firsthand. While living in Oklahoma, he had studied to be a lawyer. But a new state law said that African-Americans were not allowed to take the **bar exam**, the test needed to become a lawyer. James Hughes had worked hard preparing for the exam, and he was very disappointed by the new law.

James Hughes was not only disappointed—he was also bitter. He was a very smart man who felt the United States was keeping him from earning a good living. Shortly after Langston was born, his father moved to Cuba and then to Mexico. James hoped to leave racism and unfairness behind him.

In the meantime, he and his wife had not been getting along well. So Carrie and Langston remained in the United States. They moved around a lot while Carrie looked for work and often lived with her mother in Lawrence, Kansas.

When Langston was about five years old, his parents tried to make their marriage work again. Carrie and Langston traveled to Mexico City, Mexico, to live with James Hughes. Soon after their arrival, however, a huge earthquake shook the city, and Carrie was terrified. By then she had decided that her marriage was over. So she and her son said good-bye to James and traveled back to the United States.

LANGSTON HUGHES'S GRANDMOTHER, MARY LANGSTON. SHE HELPED RAISE
AND CARE FOR LANGSTON FOR SEVERAL YEARS.

Langston and his mother moved to Topeka, Kansas. Carrie had been offered a job there, and it was time for Langston to start school. Carrie came from a well-educated family. Many of her relatives were well-known leaders in the struggle for African-American rights. She insisted that Langston attend the all-white school near their home, rather than the black school across town. Langston proved to be a very smart child and a good student. Some of the white teachers were kind to him. Others, however, said hateful things about him and people of his race. First grade turned out to be a difficult time for Langston. Carrie thought he might be better off in Lawrence, so she sent him to live with his grandmother.

Life in Lawrence was lonely for Langston Hughes. His grandmother, Mary Langston, was a strong, remarkable woman. She taught him about racial pride. But she was also very poor. As she aged, she became withdrawn and quiet. She wanted Langston to come straight home from school each day—and stay inside. She did this to protect him from the increasing racism in Lawrence. Sitting in a silent house, however, was hard on the young boy. Soon Langston turned to books to ease his loneliness, and those books deeply influenced him as he grew up.

When Langston was thirteen, his grandmother died. The Reeds, a couple who had long been friends with Mary, took him in. Langston enjoyed his time with the Reeds, and they were very loving toward him. Only two years later, Langston's life changed again. His mother had remarried, so he had a new stepfather—Homer Clark. Homer and Carrie asked Langston to come and live with them in Lincoln, Illinois.

Langston was excited about this move. Over the years, he had missed his mother terribly. He did well in school in Lincoln and liked having a stepbrother (Homer's son from a previous marriage). But Langston's life was still not settled. Homer and Carrie soon moved to Cleveland, and Langston found himself in another new school.

Then, after his sophomore year in high school, Langston's mother separated from Homer and moved to Chicago. Langston went with her and spent the summer working. Carrie wanted Langston to quit school altogether and work full-time. That idea did not appeal to the young man, so he returned to Cleveland on his own.

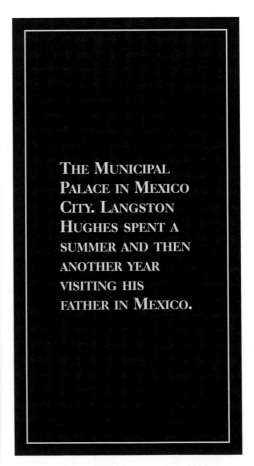

THE MUNICIPAL PALACE IN MEXICO CITY. LANGSTON HUGHES SPENT A SUMMER AND THEN ANOTHER YEAR VISITING HIS FATHER IN MEXICO.

Only a teenager, Langston lived by himself in a **boardinghouse** and returned to his high school. There he excelled as a student. He also ran track and joined a number of clubs. But most important, Langston continued to read and appreciate books. Inspired by poets such as Carl Sandburg and Walt Whitman, Langston also began writing. Many of his poems and stories were published in the high school magazine.

At the end of Langston's junior year in high school, Carrie returned to Cleveland. She and Homer Clark got back together, and Langston began living with them again. Then Langston received a message from James Hughes, inviting him to spend the summer in Mexico. Langston agreed and was thrilled by the chance to see his father again.

He did not know what his father was really like, though. That summer, Langston lived in Mexico and learned to speak Spanish. But his biggest discovery was that his father was an angry, difficult man. James put Langston to work and criticized him at every turn. Langston was happy to return to Cleveland.

POET WALT WHITMAN. AS A YOUNG MAN, LANGSTON HUGHES WAS INFLUENCED BY WHITMAN AND OTHER FINE WRITERS.

BOATS TRAVELING THE MISSISSIPPI RIVER. IT WAS THIS BODY OF WATER THAT INSPIRED HUGHES TO WRITE "THE NEGRO SPEAKS OF RIVERS," HIS FIRST WELL-KNOWN POEM.

After Langston Hughes graduated from high school with honors, he knew he wanted to be a writer. But he also knew that a good writer needs a good education. The only person in his family who could afford college tuition was James Hughes. So Langston got on a train and headed back to Mexico. His father could be difficult, but he was Langston's only chance.

As Langston Hughes rode the train along the Mississippi River, he was inspired by the great body of water. As he stared at the mighty Mississippi, he thought about his past and his future. He began writing, and before long he had written a poem titled "The Negro Speaks of Rivers." That poem would change his life.

Once in Mexico, Langston Hughes spoke to his father about his desire to attend Columbia University in New York City. He told him about his wish to be a writer. James Hughes thought these ideas were nonsense. He was happy to pay for his son's education, but he wanted him to attend school in Switzerland and study engineering.

When Langston refused, his father decided not to send him to college or pay his fare back home. Instead, Langston was stuck in Mexico. Rather than be angry, the young man used that time to write. He began sending poems, stories, and plays to a children's magazine called *The Brownies' Book.* This magazine had been founded by W. E. B. Du Bois, a civil rights activist Langston had long admired. Jessie Fauset, the editor of *The Brownies' Book,* liked Langston's writing and was happy to publish his work.

W. E. B. DU BOIS WAS A RESPECTED CIVIL RIGHTS ACTIVIST AND EDITOR OF THE *CRISIS,* A MAGAZINE THAT PUBLISHED SOME OF HUGHES'S FIRST POEMS.

Then Langston submitted "The Negro Speaks of Rivers." Fauset thought the poem was beautiful, and she had it published in the *Crisis*, another magazine founded by Du Bois. But the *Crisis* was not a children's publication. It was a serious magazine aimed at adults. Du Bois was most impressed with Hughes's writing. He asked to see more of Langston's poems.

When James Hughes saw the success his son was having, he finally agreed to send him to Columbia. In August 1921, Langston Hughes boarded another train and headed to New York. Once in the big city, he was struck by the racism on the university campus. Other students ignored him or kept him out of group activities. But Hughes didn't let that stop him. He began exploring New York and enjoying the **culture** it had to offer. He met the editors at the *Crisis*, and he went to plays and poetry readings. He realized there was a great big world he had not yet seen. So after a year at Columbia, he withdrew. He decided it was time to work and to travel. It was time to get an education about life.

THE *CRISIS* WAS AN IMPORTANT PUBLICATION FOR THE AFRICAN-AMERICAN COMMUNITY, AND IT WELCOMED THE WORK OF LANGSTON HUGHES.

NEW YORK CITY WAS AN EXCITING PLACE IN THE 1920s. HUGHES ATTENDED COLUMBIA UNIVERSITY BRIEFLY BUT SOON DECIDED TO TRAVEL THE WORLD.

After working at a handful of odd jobs in the New York area, Hughes had another idea. He got a job in the kitchen of a freight ship headed to Senegal in Africa. To understand his race and his roots, he decided he needed to see Africa.

Hughes saw the beauty of Africa as well as the **poverty** that many of its people lived in. He spoke with the Africans and saw all that he could of their homeland. And throughout his travels, he continued to write and submit his work to the *Crisis*.

LANGSTON HUGHES EXPERIENCED THE BEAUTY OF AFRICA AND SPOKE WITH ITS PEOPLE. HIS TRIP TO THE CONTINENT HELPED HIM BETTER UNDERSTAND HIS AFRICAN-AMERICAN ROOTS.

After visiting thirty-two ports in Africa, Hughes got a job on a ship headed for the Netherlands. After that, he traveled to Paris. There he got a job in the kitchen of the Grand Duc, a nightclub. Hughes loved the jazz music he heard at the club. And in his writing, he began to work in the rhythms and the sounds of the music.

While in Paris, Hughes had a brief romance with a young woman named Anne-Marie Coussey. For a time, they talked about getting married. But Coussey, who was impressed with Hughes's writing, pushed him to finish college. Hughes did not want to be pushed, and soon the relationship ended. After that, he spent some time in Italy and then returned to the United States.

THE MOULIN ROUGE WAS ONE OF MANY NIGHTCLUBS THAT THRIVED IN PARIS. HUGHES ENJOYED HIS TIME IN THAT CITY AND GOT A JOB AT ANOTHER NIGHTCLUB, THE GRAND DUC.

In 1924, back in New York, Langston Hughes found himself in an interesting time. The **Harlem Renaissance** had begun, and his writings in the *Crisis* had made him well known. All sorts of opportunities awaited him.

HARLEM'S LAFAYETTE THEATER IN **1927**. DURING THE HARLEM RENAISSANCE, THIS NEW YORK CITY NEIGHBORHOOD WAS A LIVELY PLACE WHERE THE BLACK CULTURE WAS CELEBRATED.

The Renaissance and Beyond

While Langston Hughes had been traveling, he had become well known in the United States. Many people in the literary world saw him as a great voice of the African-American people.

At parties in Harlem, he met other writers such as Countee Cullen, Claude McKay, Zora Neale Hurston, and James Weldon Johnson. He spoke with Charles Johnson, editor of a magazine called *Opportunity*. And he enjoyed the nightlife in Harlem.

DURING THE 1920s, LANGSTON HUGHES BECAME WELL KNOWN IN HARLEM AND THROUGHOUT THE WORLD. HE SPENT TIME WITH OTHER WRITERS AND ARTISTS, AND HE ENJOYED THE NIGHTLIFE OF THE HARLEM RENAISSANCE.

During this **decade**, known as the Roaring Twenties, black culture was celebrated. The musical styles of blues and jazz were popular. People were dancing the Charleston.

A novelist and critic named Carl Van Vechten often attended the same parties as Hughes did. Van Vechten was impressed with Hughes's talent and helped get his first book published. It was a collection of poetry called *The Weary Blues.* In these poems, Hughes often spoke of the loneliness he would feel his entire life. He was popular among other writers and artists, but he always felt separated from other people.

Although he loved New York City life, Hughes could not afford to live there. So he moved to Washington, D.C., to live with his mother. While there, he worked as a hotel busboy and had an interesting encounter. A well-known poet named Vachel Lindsay was staying at the hotel. When Lindsay was dining in the hotel restaurant one day, Hughes gave him some of his poems and a note.

CARL VAN VECHTEN WAS A NOVELIST AND CRITIC WHO HELPED HUGHES GET HIS FIRST BOOK PUBLISHED.

Lindsay was thrilled by the poems and presented some at his next public reading. Newspapers across the country stated that a new talent had been discovered.

By 1926, Hughes decided he wanted to go back to college. He enrolled in Lincoln University, an all-black college near Oxford, Pennsylvania. At age twenty-four, he was older than most of the other students. But he enjoyed his classmates as well as his studies.

The following year, another book of his poems was published. Called *Fine Clothes to the Jew*, the work was mis-understood by some critics of the time. But today, it is considered one of his most important. Its title refers to poor African-Americans having to take their valued possessions to pawnshops, which were often owned by Jewish people.

LANGSTON HUGHES AT LINCOLN UNIVERSITY. AT AGE TWENTY-FOUR, HUGHES ENROLLED AT THIS ALL-BLACK COLLEGE IN PENNSYLVANIA, AND HE EARNED HIS DEGREE IN 1929.

Hughes continued to attend college in Pennsylvania, but nearly every weekend he took the train to New York City. He still loved the nightlife and the culture. And he also had a new friend—an elderly widow named Charlotte Osgood Mason. Mason agreed to be Hughes's **patron**. She gave him money each month to encourage his writing. Hughes appreciated the help, and he spent much time with her.

Unfortunately, getting help from Mason was a mixed blessing. She sometimes criticized his work. She felt it was her right to voice her opinion because she was giving him money. The arrangement was hard for Hughes. He began writing less and spent his time on other things.

In June 1929, Hughes graduated from college, and soon the world changed again. In October 1929, the stock market crashed, and the **Great Depression** began. The Roaring Twenties came to an end. And the Harlem Renaissance was over.

CHARLOTTE OSGOOD MASON WAS AN IMPORTANT PERSON IN HUGHES'S LIFE. FOR SEVERAL YEARS, SHE WAS HIS PATRON AND SUPPORTED HIM FINANCIALLY. BUT OVER TIME, HUGHES REALIZED THAT HE NEEDED TO WRITE WITHOUT HER HELP.

In spite of the problems Hughes was having with his writing, he did manage a few projects. He and Zora Neale Hurston wrote a play called *Mule Bone* together. He also continued to work on a novel, *Not without Laughter,* which was loosely based on his life as a young man. The book was published in 1930, and many critics showered praise on Hughes.

In the meantime, Hughes had grown tired of Mason's control. She felt that he was ungrateful to her. So their financial arrangement and friendship both came to an end. At about the same time, Hughes and Hurston had an argument that ended their friendship. Hughes realized it was time to make it on his own as a writer.

During the spring of 1930, Hughes had traveled to Cuba. There he learned more about Caribbean and Latin American music. And he met important Cuban poets, including Nicolás Guillén.

ZORA NEALE HURSTON COLLABORATED WITH HUGHES ON A PLAY CALLED *MULE BONE.* HURSTON WAS A TALENTED WRITER, BUT HER FRIENDSHIP WITH HUGHES ENDED AFTER AN ARGUMENT.

After parting with Mason, Hughes won a prize for his writing. With the prize money, he returned to Cuba in 1931 and then sailed to Haiti. He and Haitian poet Jacques Roumain spent time together discussing their countries and their work. The two men became lifelong friends.

After leaving Cuba, Hughes traveled through the South on his way back to New York. He made a stop at Bethune-Cookman College in Florida and had a wonderful meeting with Mary McLeod Bethune. The college president praised Hughes for his writing, but she urged him to do more. She encouraged him to take his poetry to the people. She felt that he had much to say and that the people of America needed to hear him.

MARY MCLEOD BETHUNE WAS PRESIDENT OF BETHUNE-COOKMAN COLLEGE IN FLORIDA. SHE ENCOURAGED HUGHES TO TOUR THE COUNTRY AND SHARE HIS POETRY WITH THE PUBLIC.

A Man to Remember

Once back in New York, Langston Hughes began to voice his political views more. He wrote for a magazine called *New Masses,* and he associated with many members of the Communist Party. Though he claimed never to be a **communist** himself, he agreed with communists on many issues. Communism was often viewed negatively in the United States, but the ideas of communism appealed to some African-Americans. In theory, racism, unemployment, poverty, and hunger did not exist under communism. Some African-Americans felt that everyone was treated equally under communism. And equality was something they did not experience in the United States.

In the meantime, Langston Hughes began making plans to follow Mary McLeod Bethune's advice. He received a **grant** that awarded him a substantial amount of money. And he published a collection of poems called *The Negro Mother and Other Dramatic Recitations.* Then he set out to bring his poetry to the people.

NEW MASSES WAS A MAGAZINE ASSOCIATED WITH THE COMMUNIST PARTY. LANGSTON HUGHES OFTEN WROTE FOR THIS PUBLICATION, AND FOR A TIME HE WAS INTRIGUED BY COMMUNIST IDEAS.

He and Radcliffe Lucas, a college friend, left New York by car in November 1931. They toured Pennsylvania, giving poetry readings along the way, and then headed south. Hughes realized he had to be careful in the southern states because they could be dangerous places for black men. Racial violence was not uncommon. For one reading in Chapel Hill, North Carolina, Hughes even had police protection.

For weeks, the tour through South Carolina, Florida, Georgia, Alabama, Tennessee, and other states continued. Then Hughes went to Oklahoma, Kansas, Missouri, and Texas. Finally the tour headed to Arizona and New Mexico. In the spring of 1932, it ended in California.

During these months, Langston Hughes touched the lives of many people. He brought his words to them, offering his feelings and his ideas. He did more than sell books and see the country— he gave himself to his audiences.

LANGSTON HUGHES WITH RADCLIFFE LUCAS (LEFT). IN 1931 AND 1932, THESE MEN TRAVELED BY CAR AND PRESENTED HUGHES'S POETRY AT PUBLIC READINGS.

While still in California, Hughes worked on a children's book with his friend Arna Bontemps. *Paste Board Bandits* was published in 1935 and received wonderful reviews.

After his tour of the United States, Hughes and his longtime friend Louise Thompson were offered jobs in the Soviet Union. They planned to write a movie that was to be filmed there. This was an exciting opportunity for both of them, because no black Americans wrote movies in Hollywood.

Unfortunately, the project had many problems that could not be solved. So the film company canceled the film.

To make up for the disappointment, the company offered Hughes and the other Americans a tour of Russia. Hughes got to see all of Asia as well as Russia. On his trip, he met a young woman named Sylvia Chen. They discussed marriage for some time, but the wedding never took place. And in the summer of 1933, Hughes returned to the United States.

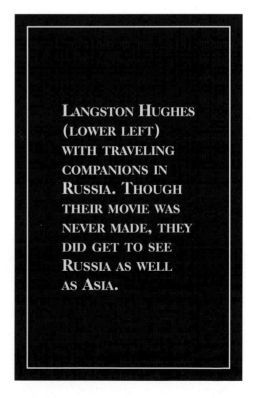

LANGSTON HUGHES (LOWER LEFT) WITH TRAVELING COMPANIONS IN RUSSIA. THOUGH THEIR MOVIE WAS NEVER MADE, THEY DID GET TO SEE RUSSIA AS WELL AS ASIA.

LANGSTON HUGHES WITH TOY HARPER AT HER APARTMENT. HUGHES LIVED WITH TOY AND HER HUSBAND, EMERSON, FOR VARIOUS PERIODS IN HIS LIFE.

At that time, Hughes began living in Carmel, California. There he worked on a series of stories about the relationships of blacks and whites. The book, titled *The Ways of White Folks*, was published in 1934. While in California, Hughes also became active in the John Reed Club, a communist group that had a chapter in Carmel.

In December 1934, Hughes learned that his father had died. He traveled to Mexico City to settle his father's estate. Although the two men had not seen one another since 1921, Langston always felt controlled by James. In some ways, Langston accepted his father's death with a sense of relief.

While in Mexico, Langston was awarded another grant. With this money, he began work on a new novel. But he soon turned his attention to writing plays.

After a trip to Europe in 1937, Hughes returned to New York in early 1938. There, he and Louise Thompson founded the Harlem Suitcase Theater. During this time, he shared an apartment with family friends, Toy and Emerson Harper. Hughes lived with them on and off for many years. In 1940, he worked on the script for a film called *Way Down South*. Hughes found Hollywood to be an unpleasant place and never worked as a scriptwriter again.

LOUISE THOMPSON, A RESPECTED WRITER WHO ALSO RECEIVED SUPPORT FROM PATRON CHARLOTTE MASON FOR A TIME. THOMPSON AND HUGHES FOUNDED THE HARLEM SUITCASE THEATER TOGETHER.

During World War II (1939–1945), Hughes was very productive. He wrote his autobiography, *The Big Sea*, and he supported the American war effort. He wrote lyrics for advertisements to buy **war bonds**. He also wrote articles for many newspapers about the war. In 1949, his opera libretto for *Troubled Island* was performed in New York City. Critics praised the production as well as Hughes's work.

Hughes also wrote a great deal of poetry during the 1940s, including the collections *Shakespeare in Harlem* and *Fields of Wonder.* In 1951, *Montage of a Dream Deferred* was published. Many consider this to be Hughes's finest work.

In the 1950s, Langston Hughes faced problems of a political nature. U.S. senator Joseph McCarthy headed a committee to find communists in America. The goal of the group was to expose people who were not loyal to American **democracy**. At this time, many accused communists were **blacklisted** throughout the country. Before Hughes appeared in front of the committee, he thought long and hard about communism. He had come to realize that Soviets could be racist, too. And he had come to see that in communist countries creativity was often controlled by the government. He explained to the committee that he used to have communist beliefs. But he was not forced to name anyone else from the communist groups. This was a relief for Hughes. Many other people had been put in jail for not naming people they suspected of communism. Even Hughes's **literary agent**, Max Lieber, left the country because he feared having to hand over names to the committee.

In the years to come, Hughes produced a remarkable amount of work. He wrote books for children as well as collections of poetry. He also wrote a weekly newspaper column for the *Chicago Defender* and then for the *New York Post*. In these columns, he often featured a character named Jesse B. Semple (sometimes called "Simple"). This character went on to appear in books as well as in a play called *Simply Heavenly.*

In 1960, Langston Hughes received the Spingarn Medal. This award is the highest honor given by African-Americans to an African-American. Hughes was deeply touched by the honor. The next year, he was inducted into the National Institute of Arts and Letters. He was only the second African-American to receive this honor, which recognized his important contribution to American literature. (The first African-American inductee was W. E. B. Du Bois.) In the following years, he wrote the plays *Gospel Glow* and *Tambourines to Glory*. These plays illustrate the influence of **gospel** music on African-American religion.

Hughes began to feel ill in the spring of 1967. He checked into a New York City hospital under the name James Hughes and stayed there for a few weeks. Doctors determined that he suffered from heart disease as well as cancer. They operated on him, but it was too late.

LANGSTON HUGHES IN THE SPOTLIGHT AT THE 1960 SPINGARN MEDAL CEREMONY. RECEIVING THIS AWARD WAS AN IMPORTANT MOMENT IN HUGHES'S LIFE.

On May 22, 1967, Langston Hughes died. In his will, he had specified the kind of funeral he wished to have. His funeral was held in Harlem with a jazz band. Arna Bontemps spoke about Hughes and read some of his poems. It was a celebration of his extraordinary life.

After the funeral, Hughes's body was cremated as a group of friends read aloud the "The Negro Speaks of Rivers." Twenty-four years later, on his eighty-ninth birthday, Hughes's ashes were moved to New York City's Schomburg Center for Research in Black Culture. The burial spot is marked by a floor tile called "Rivers." The tile was designed to remember Langston Hughes and all that he gave to American literature.

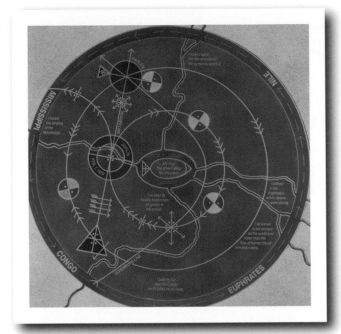

THE ORIGINAL ARTWORK USED FOR THE "RIVERS" TILE AT THE SCHOMBURG CENTER FOR RESEARCH IN BLACK CULTURE. LANGSTON HUGHES'S ASHES WERE MOVED TO THAT SPOT TWENTY-FOUR YEARS AFTER HIS DEATH.

Timeline

1902	James Langston Hughes is born on February 1 in Joplin, Missouri.
1903	Langston Hughes's father moves to Mexico.
1909	Hughes begins living with his grandmother, Mary Langston.
1915	Langston Hughes's grandmother, Mary Langston, dies.
1919	Hughes spends a summer in Mexico with his father.
1921	"The Negro Speaks of Rivers" is published, and Hughes enrolls at Columbia University in New York City.
1922	Hughes quits college and begins working at odd jobs and traveling.
1924	Hughes returns to the United States.
1926	*The Weary Blues*, Hughes's first book, is published, and he enrolls at Lincoln University.
1929	Hughes graduates from college.
1931	Hughes begins a poetry tour of the United States.
1932	Hughes travels to the Soviet Union and Asia.
1938	With Louise Thompson, Hughes founds the Harlem Suitcase Theater.
1943	Hughes creates the character Jesse B. Semple.
1953	Hughes testifies before Senator McCarthy's committee.
1960	Hughes receives the Spingarn Medal.
1961	Hughes is inducted into the National Institute of Arts and Letters.
1967	Langston Hughes dies on May 22 in New York City.
1991	Hughes's ashes are moved to the Schomburg Center for Research in Black Culture.

Glossary

bar exam (BAR ig-ZAM)
The bar exam is a test that a person must pass to be allowed to work as a lawyer in a particular state.

blacklisted (BLAK-list-ed)
To be blacklisted means to be excluded from groups or from employment.

blues (BLOOZ)
Blues is a type of music that is often marked by sad and slow lyrics.

boardinghouse (BOHR-ding-hows)
A boardinghouse is a house where people can live and have meals provided.

communist (KOM-yuh-nist)
A communist is a person who believes in communism, a system in which the government owns everything.

culture (KUHL-chur)
The culture of a community includes fine arts such as theater, literature, and visual arts.

decade (DEK-ayd)
A decade is a period of ten years.

democracy (di-MOK-ruh-see)
A democracy is a government in which people vote for their leaders.

gospel (GOSS-puhl)
Gospel music is marked by religious lyrics.

grant (GRANT)
A grant is money given for a special purpose, such as writing a book or studying a certain subject.

Great Depression (GRAYT di-PRESH-uhn)
The Great Depression was a period in U.S. history marked by unemployment, poverty, and homelessness.

Harlem Renaissance (HAR-lum REN-uh-sahnss)
The Harlem Renaissance was an era in the 1920s marked by great artistic activity among African-Americans.

jazz (JAZ)
Jazz is a type of music known for its various rhythms and improvisation.

librettos (lih-BREH-tohs)
Librettos are books that contain the texts of musical theater works such as operas.

literary agent (LIT-uh-rehr-ee AY-juhnt)
A literary agent plans, makes deals, and handles contracts for writers.

patron (PAY-truhn)
A patron is someone who gives money or other assistance to help support a cause.

poverty (POV-ur-tee)
Someone who lives in poverty has little money and owns very few possessions.

racism (RAY-sism)
Racism is a belief that one race is better than others.

segregated (SEG-ruh-gayt-ed)
A group of people who are segregated are kept apart from other groups of people.

war bonds (WOR BONDZ)
War bonds are investments that support a war effort.

Index

FOR FURTHER READING

Books

Dunham, Montrew. *Langston Hughes: Young Black Poet.* New York: Aladdin, 1995.

Hughes, Langston. *The Dream Keeper and Other Poems.* New York: Knopf, 1996.

Meltzer, Milton. *Langston Hughes.* Brookfield, Conn.: Millbrook Press, 1997.

Walker, Alice. *Langston Hughes: American Poet.* New York: HarperCollins Children's Books, 2002.

Web Sites

Visit our homepage for lots of links about the Langston Hughes:
http://www.childsworld.com/links.html

Note to Parents, Teachers, and Librarians:
We routinely verify our Web links to make sure they're safe,
active sites—so encourage your readers to check them out!

ABOUT THE AUTHOR

Lucia Raatma received her bachelor's degree in English literature from the University of South Carolina and her master's degree in cinema studies from New York University. After spending many years in Manhattan book publishing, she turned her interests to freelance writing, and she has since written a wide range of books for young people. When she is not researching or writing, she enjoys going to movies, playing tennis, practicing yoga, and spending time with her husband, daughter, and golden retriever. She lives in New York.